WINGS No 4

F-111 Aard\ /\ R

Hans Halberstadt

Windrow & Greene

© 1992 Windrow & Greene Ltd.

Published in Great Britain 1992 by
Windrow & Greene Ltd.
5 Gerrard Street
London W1V 7LJ

A CIP catalogue record for this book is
available from the British Library.

ISBN 1-872004-42-3

Published in the USA by
Specialty Press Publishers
& Wholesalers Inc.
PO Box 338
Stillwater, MN 55082
(612) 430-2210/800-888-9653

Dedication:
For Veronica, for service above and
beyond the call of duty

Acknowledgements:
Many thanks to the 27th Tactical
Fighter Wing at Cannon Air Force
Base, New Mexico. A salute to Col.
Arnold Franklin, Major Rick Olson,
Airman Shawn Ankrom, and the crew
at headquarters and the Public Affairs
shop; to Lt.Col. John Hill, Major Tom
Yanni and Capt. Bill Leake at the 524th
TFS; to Capt. Brinley at the 522nd TFS;
and to all the folks at Cannon who
helped get this thing off the ground.
Likewise, a salute to Capt. Kevin
Baggett at Tactical Air Command PAO
for his usual friendly assistance.
Hans Halberstadt
San Jose, California
February 1992

(Title page) All dressed up, with
someplace to go – and the radios
decide to quit. An elderly D model
with an impatient crew waits, with
engines running, at the arming area
for an avionics specialist to swap one
big black box for another (hopefully,
operative). Such last-minute repairs
are normally effective, and the happy
couple will probably make it to the
ball before midnight.

Greys, greens and browns merge on
the ramp at Cannon AFB at the start
of another day's flying for the 27th
Tactical Fighter Wing. Although the
new 'wraparound' slate grey scheme
gives the foreground F-111s an
air of modernity, the aircraft are
essentially no different from the other
Aardvarks ranged beyond.

1: Attack of the Aardvark

ight, 3 February 1991, near Baghdad, Iraq. A composite 'strike package' of F-111Fs, supported by F-16s for air cap, F-4G Wild Weasels for lethal suppression of enemy air defences, and EF-111 'Sparkvarks' for enemy radar suppression, drive in to their primary target in the opening rounds of the Gulf War: a chemical weapons facility deep inside a high threat area. A weather front moves in, but the strike package press on, trying to beat the clouds but thinking seriously about the likelihood of a diversion to an alternate. Capt. 'Jazz' Griffin leads one of the flights of four.

The attack track comes up from the south-east; they press on through gathering weather. Just short of the target Capt. Griffin's right-seater detects a SAM launch directly below – a flash followed by what looks like a telephone pole accelerating to high speed. Griffin takes evasive action, turning hard toward the missile by instinctive defensive reaction. At a bank angle of about 135 degrees and 10 degrees nose low he gets inside the missile track; the SAM detonates just astern of the F-111. Griffin and his WSO (Weapon System Officer) see the silhouette of their own airplane before them, outlined in brilliant orange light as the warhead explodes. The aircraft is rocked violently, but is recovered 7,000 ft lower.

The crew elect to press on to the target, but find themselves stuck in a band of heavy flak 30 seconds out from the release point. All the thrashing around has wasted the WSO's previous efforts at a bombing solution, so he works frantically to get set up to drop from the new altitude. But the target is completely obscured, and Griffin 'safes' his GBU-24 bombs; he also announces that he's heading for the alternate target. Despite the lack of support at the alternate, and despite the encounter with the SAM site, Griffin hears the laconic voices of his flight accept the invitation: 'Two', 'Three', 'Four'.

The flight climbs back to its assigned altitude and heads for the alternate target, an airfield to the east. They attack, with the enemy air defences becoming ever more intense as the parade of F-111s roars overhead. The targets are destroyed; none of the Aardvarks is hit; and the flight returns home. Griffin gets a Distinguished Flying Cross, and the others are also decorated.

'The F-111 is probably the best weapon we have available now', says Capt. Griffin. 'It does so much, has such good penetration capability, and has the best air-to-ground package we can put on something right now. It leaves a lot of room for error – a lot of reaction parameters. In a wartime environment, when you have to move the aircraft – you move the aircraft! With the F-111 you can be off the primary parameters a little and still get that bomb to do its job. There are very few bombs we can't carry and there are very few jobs we can't do.'

It probably surprised the people who criticized the '111 during its formative years – if they still cared – that the Aardvark turned out to be one of the most capable, reliable and effective weapons systems in the US arsenal. Back in the 1960s and '70s few would have guessed it.

The design was born as the TFX (tactical fighter, experimental) during the Kennedy administration. The initial contract was awarded to General Dynamics in November 1962, and called for a fighter/bomber that would be suitable for both the US Air Force and the Navy, with variable sweep wings, Mach 2.5 speed, and a large payload. It was supposed to do everything, for everybody, at low cost.

As the programme evolved the costs increased dramatically; and after a long sequence of delays and

'Okay, buddy, that's as far as you're going for the moment'. After successfully getting out of the blocks, an Aardvark trundles down the taxiway to be inspected by a multitude of attendants, weighed, and pronounced capable of sustained flight.

overruns, of added weight, and the abandonment of the programme by the Navy (who had committed to buy 1,300) and the British, the media began a feeding frenzy. Finally the first aircraft were delivered, and sent to show their stuff over the jungles of Viet Nam in March 1968. Three of the eight deployed crashed in the first two-week period – without any help from the enemy. Fifteen were lost over the next two years to mechanical failure: not an auspicious beginning.

Somehow the design struggled on through an awkward and sometimes troublesome adolescence, to be refined and upgraded, strengthened and improved, rather than discarded. It has emerged as a strong, reliable, effective and mature weapon system.

Despite the media attention lavished on other airframes like the F-16, the Tornado, or even the A-10, the Aardvark managed to put more iron effectively on target than any other system in the Gulf War. It can carry more, farther, lower, faster – in the middle of the night, through the smoke of a thousand fires, under the radars of enemy defences – and still plant its cargo where it is supposed to go. It does this job better than the sleek, fly-by-wire 'electric jets' and Strike Eagles, by being a good idea brought to full maturity. And despite the age of the airframes (even the newest of which are nearly 20 years old), the Aardvark is destined to soldier on for another decade or two in the service of its country.

Under a chilly winter storm front an Aardvark leaves its pen on Cannon's long flight line, headed out with three litter-mates for a few hours' freedom in the low-level skies of eastern New Mexico. The aircraft's powerful AN/APQ-130 radar would roast the photographer if it were energized, but it is normally secured until well airborne. When it is tested on the ground before taxi, the pilots turn on the landing light as a warning to avoid the front of the aeroplane.

Most bombing practice is done with modest 25 lb 'Blue Bombs', a dozen of which are stored in a BDU-33 unit on the inboard wing pylons. They may not seem very intimidating here, but you still don't want one falling on you: the arming area checks are done with the same thorough attention to detail that would be used for big 2,000 lb 'pig iron' devices.

Ten degrees of 'alpha', accelerating through 150 knots, and with a positive rate of climb established: it is time to retract gear and flaps, lower the nose a little, and work the airspeed up to about Mach .75 for a 'plain vanilla' version of an F-111 take-off. Single-ship departures are the norm, formation take-offs the exception. This Aardvark displaying the yellow fin stripe of the 524th TFTS is off for a couple of hours' work-out at the Melrose Bombing Range.

The tower at Cannon is an equal opportunity employer: here a female member of the air traffic control crew helps weave the take-offs into a safe pattern in the morning skies over New Mexico.

The Aardvark's wing is a marvellous
device, and hardly ever falls off
anymore. Full forward, with leading
edge extensions and flaps out, it is
tremendously efficient, and permits
leisurely approaches and departures
even with a full cargo of internal and
external stores.

Out over the Atlantic an old FB-111A of the 509th Bomb Wing out of Pease AFB, New Hampshire, cruises serenely toward a distant tanker rendezvous. A large internal fuel capacity, along with aerial refuelling and the two-man crew, make the F-111 a good candidate for deep-penetration missions like the attack on Libya in 1986. *(Ken Hammond/ USAF/Arms Communications)*

A Pease-based FB-111 unloads a stick of Mk 82 high-drag bombs. The parachutes retard the ordnance, allowing the aircraft to make a clean getaway before impact. *(Ken Hammond/USAF/Arms Communications)*

The Aardvark is most efficient up at altitude, and typically cruises at about 25,000 ft when fuel economy is an issue and threats are not. *(Ken Hammond/USAF/Arms Communications)*

In the break, a '111 drops into the pattern at Cannon after a trying afternoon on the bombing range. Contrails form from the wingtips when moisture is present in the air; sometimes, under higher G loads, little clouds form at the wing roots as well.

Jets depart at 20-second intervals, form up in pairs and flights-of-four, and climb to their assigned altitude for transit to the training route. Upon returning to the base the aircraft announce their arrival by flying a tight formation along the centreline at height, before 'pitching out' and landing at predetermined intervals.

Short final: it's attitude, not airspeed, that gets an F-111 safely back to earth. Maintain ten units of 'alpha' (angle of attack), wings full forward, flaps full down, and you will be sliding over the threshold at about 130 knots indicated; the wheels will slam back aboard about 500 ft down the line, leaving about 9,500 ft to bring the speed down enough to make the turn on to the taxiway.

Does this look like a Mach 2.5+ machine to you? Don't try this configuration with the throttles forward – the flaps would rip right off, and maybe the wings as well. The aeroplane and the wing owe a lot to the original concept of the system as a multi-service fighter/bomber. The wing, flaps, leading edge extensions, and 'cast iron' landing gear were all designed to the robust standards of carrier-based aircraft, which are not so much landed as crashed on a designated spot and dragged away.

A Delta is guided back to its pen after a few hours on the loose by an attentive 27th Tactical Fighter Wing crew chief. The enlisted men and women are the unsung heroes of most combat aviation units; they spend entire careers getting the birds launched and recovered safely, work horrendous hours when required – and never, ever, get a ride. The lack of glory is not because pilots or commanders don't try to get them recognition: the officers are all quick to acknowledge that the missions would be a 'no go' without the dedication of the ground crews.

As soon as the engines are secured and the pins back in the ejection seat handles, maintenance people scramble aboard for inspections, service, and the dozens of routine checks required after each mission.

2: Walkaround

It's a tight little cockpit but you really can get two guys in there, and they each get a door of their own. Visibility is restricted, but it's a bomber, not a fighter, so that's not such a problem. Those long, sloping windscreens in front are thick laminated glass, but the occasional bird still manages to punch through them.

The F-111, despite its age and comparatively antique technologies, still retains unique talents and capabilities. It is sneaky, like the F-117, but avoids radar detection by its tactics rather than its technologies – and carries much more, farther and faster. It carries a bigger load than the F-15E Strike Eagle, and delivers it in all weathers, day or night, with equal precision. As the Air Force describes it, the F-111 is a long range, adverse weather, day or night aircraft. It has a variable sweep wing which, when swept fully forward, permits the aircraft to take off and land at high gross weights and moderate air speeds. With the wings swept back the aircraft achieves Mach 2.5+. It has a huge payload (up to 45,000 lbs), long range (about 3,000 nautical miles on internal fuel alone), and a very short take-off and landing capability. Its fire control systems provide the ability to engage targets effectively from low or high altitudes.

Unlike most fighter/bomber aircraft, the Aardvark is designed to be happy down on the deck, at high speeds, in conditions that make the crews of other aircraft puke. The F-111 has a dedicated set of systems for automatic terrain following that provide a safe, comfortable, hands-off ride 'over the river and through the woods' at altitudes down to 200 feet. It can fly across a thousand miles of enemy territory this way, from way point to way point, automatically, and then deliver weapons with reliable precision. Bombs can be 'tossed' more than eight miles (handy for those tactical nukes), or dropped from a dive or level flight over the target – all with great accuracy, thanks to digital computer systems that rapidly and accurately compile data and generate automatic fire control solutions.

The Aardvark is the only American military aircraft in the current inventory that does not use ejection seats. Instead, the F-111's entire cockpit (along with a bit of the wing) separates from the rest of the airframe, and the crew ride back to earth still scanning the gauges and trying to figure out what went wrong while

All fluffed up and ready for the arrival of its crew, a member of the 522nd's stable sits on the ramp before a training mission.

Another view of the cockpit canopy access panel: the handle engages a series of pins and latches that keep it firmly attached during flight ops.

descending under a big 70-ft canopy. To provide some measure of cushioning a large air bladder inflates under the capsule; on impact the bladder is designed to rupture in a controlled way. Just the same, the shock is enough to compress vertebrae – but this is better than the alternative. And if the landing is in water, the control column turns into a handle for a bilge pump. . . .

The prime contractor was General Dynamics, and the planes were assembled at the Fort Worth, Texas, plant. The F-111s are so-called 'multi-purpose fighters', although it's tough to figure out what a fighter is anymore. These 'fighters' are really multi-role bombers, able to carry virtually every conventional and 'special' weapon in the inventory – 'special' being the Air Force euphemism for tactical nuclear bombs. It also carries Sparrow and Sidewinder missiles for self defence, though this is not the aircraft in which to go brawling with MiG-29s. It is entirely possible to hang

nearly 32,000 lbs of weapons on the pylons and in the bomb bay of an Aardvark, and still get the thing off the ground; but don't expect it to be light on its feet with a load like that.

The Aardvark is propelled through the sky by a pair of Pratt & Whitney TF30 turbofans; in 'burner' they pump out 20,000+ lbs of thrust – and consume tremendous quantities of fermented dinosaur in the form of JP4 kerosene. That kind of thrust, coupled with the Aardvark's complex and capable wing design, gets the fully loaded aircraft off the runway in only 3,000 feet. If the pilot keeps the stick aft those 'leaky turbojets' will carry the Aardvark right up to Flight Level Six Zero (60,000 ft) with prompt dispatch. And with intelligent fuel management, those engines will also provide a maximum range of up to 4,100 miles on internal fuel alone (G model).

The beast is 75.5 ft from nose to tail, 17 ft from the concrete to the top of the rudder, and 63 ft from tip to

A small, jewel-like green navigation light in the starboard wing helps other aircraft identify position and direction of travel when airborne.

tip (wings extended); with the wings tucked back the spread is only 32 ft, which comes in handy for tight mountain passes. There are slight variations in the sizes of the different models – for example, the Golf version (the reworked Strategic Air Command FB-lll) has an extended wing spread of 70 ft; but they are all essentially the same basic airframe.

Until recently, F-111s served in D, E, F and EF-111A variants at RAF Upper Heyford and RAF Lakenheath in the United Kingdom, and at Mountain Home, Pease, and Cannon Air Force Bases in the United States. However, the Deltas have now completed their airframe life expectancy, and have been retired to serve as gate guards and static museum displays, or to be recycled into beer cans. The Echos and Foxtrots, along with the electronic warfare Raven, have been relocated to Cannon and the 27th Tactical Fighter Wing. The Echos can carry more than the Deltas, and deliver it with greater precision thanks to more modern avionics and fire controls.

The design has overcome its teething troubles since its first deployment to Viet Nam, and has matured into a seasoned, reliable combat veteran. In April 1986 the Aardvark was chosen to make the attack on Libya, which it did under the cover of darkness and with substantial precision. In *Desert Storm/Desert Sabre* the F-111F was an unsung hero, conducting interdiction, strategic attack and tactical ground attack missions – and writing off more than 1,500 of Saddam Hussein's armoured vehicles, trucks and tanks in the process. F-111Fs successfully took out the oil pumping stations which he used to foul the waters of the Persian Gulf, knocked down his bridges, and destroyed his communications and command facilities. The Fox model's Pave Tack system for laser designation permits great accuracy in weapon delivery. All of the F-111s are known by the official nickname 'Aardvark' (although the author has heard this affectionately modified to 'Ground Pig').

After years of debate by the official Air Force interior decorator team, this tasteful and understated grey was selected as the most suitable colour scheme for Aardvarks in the '90s. Here we see the full effect of the oh-so-subtle subdued national insignia, with brief colour accents supplied by those darling brutes at the Fighter Weapons School. Only pilots of discernment and good taste are permitted to fly these aircraft – the old, splotchy camouflage scheme being retained for the lower classes. . . .

Aardvarks allow their control surfaces to droop while parked, a breed characteristic which reveals that this one is fired up and about to go for a ride. The entire stabilizer ('stabilator', actually) moves, offering tremendous control authority for the big aircraft when its crew start 'yanking and banking'.

BOMB CAPABLE ONLY

The wing and engine intakes are full of moving parts: here the wing root and engine inlet are configured for slow speed flight.

The engine air intakes are designed – like those on most high performance fighter aircraft – to vary their shape during some flight manoeuvres. Fighter/bomber aircraft operate in extreme combinations of angle-of-attack and airspeed, conditions that would otherwise restrict airflow to the engines and could easily induce engine failure.

Another view of the starboard intake. In addition to vast quantities of air, the intakes invariably suck up the occasional bird. Sometimes, if the birds are big ones, like geese, and a lot of them are swallowed, the engine may develop indigestion – but normally this is only a problem for the birds.

Stay clear when this thing is running. The compression face of the big Pratt & Whitney TF30-P-9 is housed deep inside the fuselage where it can safely pump out nearly 20,000 lbs of thrust. Much of the air it consumes is used for cooling rather than combustion.

Resting quietly in its spot on the ramp with all electric and hydraulic power shut off, this F-111 indulges to the full its tendency to 'hang loose'.

(Above) Like the intakes, the design of the exhaust section of the engine is extremely important in providing efficient, reliable thrust under a wide spectrum of flight conditions. The aft-most section of the exhaust is actually a kind of variable nozzle that expands and contracts under engine computer control. If you stand under the approach while aircraft float in to land you will hear a series of rapid little squeals from the motors shaping this nozzle open and closed, punctuating the géntle rumble of the Pratt & Whitney.

(Right top) Despite the tremendous heat generated by the engine, these thin metal hinges controlling the nozzle are prevented from melting by use of heat-resistant alloys and vast quantities of cooling air.

(Right bottom) At the very end of the fuselage, tucked in between the engine exhausts, is the fuel dump vent. This is used in the event of an anticipated emergency landing, to discard all the fuel except the necessary minimum required to get the F-111 back on to the concrete.

High atop the starboard fin tip of an Aardvark of the 523rd TFS 'Crusaders', where it has a good view of the world astern, is the threat warning receiver and antenna components of the AN/ALQ-62 Terminal Threat Warning System. This warns the crew that somebody is lashing them with electromagnetic energy in the radar frequency bands. Sadly, it ignores a large component of the close-in threat: infrared seek and track detection and designation systems like those found on the MiG-29 and Sukhoi Su-27, and their heat-seeking AA-11 air-to-air missiles.

Four squadrons currently call Cannon AFB home, and each is distinguished by a restrained coloured namestripe on the fin – here, the red stripe of the 522nd TFS 'Fireballs'.

The leading edge extensions are extended by a rock solid rack-and-pinion system able to tolerate the heavy loads imposed by airspeeds of 250 knots on large sections of sheet metal.

The flaps use a similar system, but with a screw drive. With flaps and leading edge extensions both out the shape of the wing is radically transformed, and consequently its ability to generate lift.

(Right) This avionics bay houses the components for the right-seater's systems. A significant proportion of the total cost of the modern aeroplane – civil as well as military – goes into these unglamorous components, which are capable of such spectacular performance; most airframes, and most missions, would fail without them.

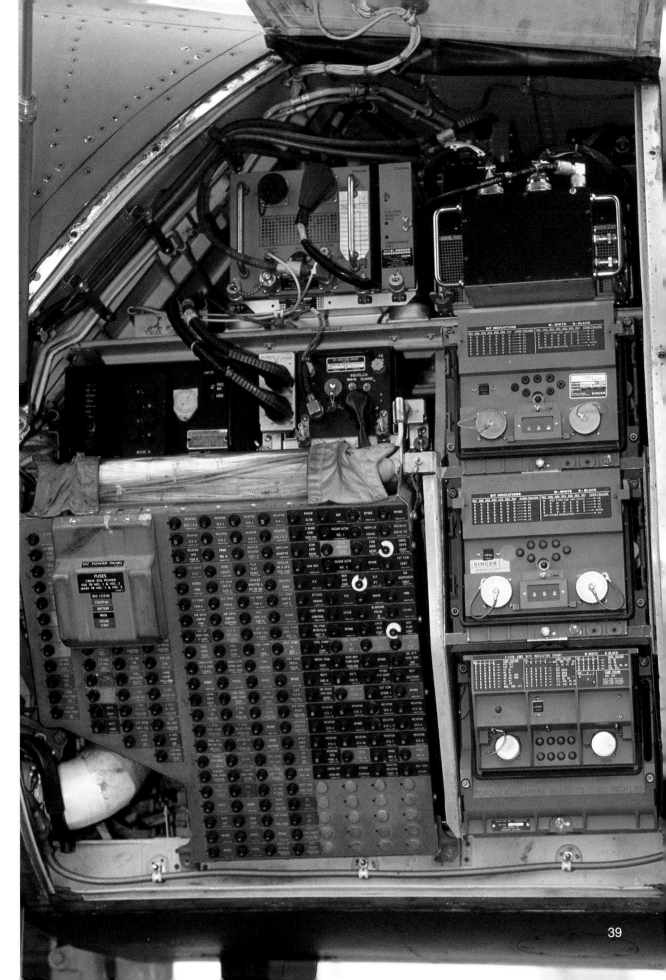

The avionics specialist undoes a couple of simple connectors, slides out a temporarily unserviceable black box (which may sometimes cost ten years of his pay), and pops in a fresh one. The ability to remove and replace defective units rapidly has a lot to do with the high mission-capable rate of even older aircraft like the F-111.

27 TFW

CANNON AFB
NM

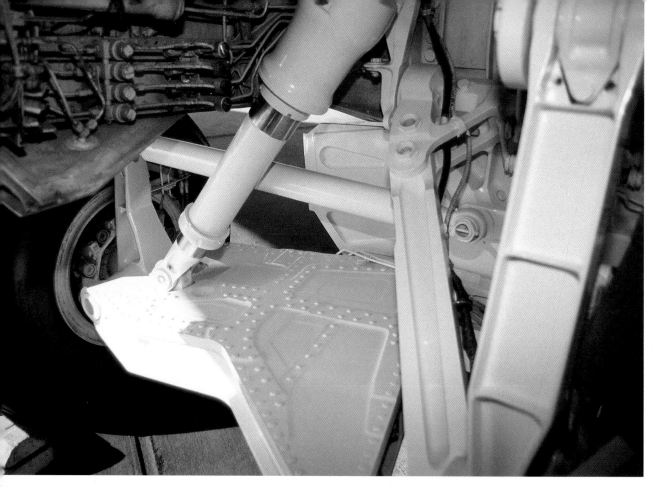

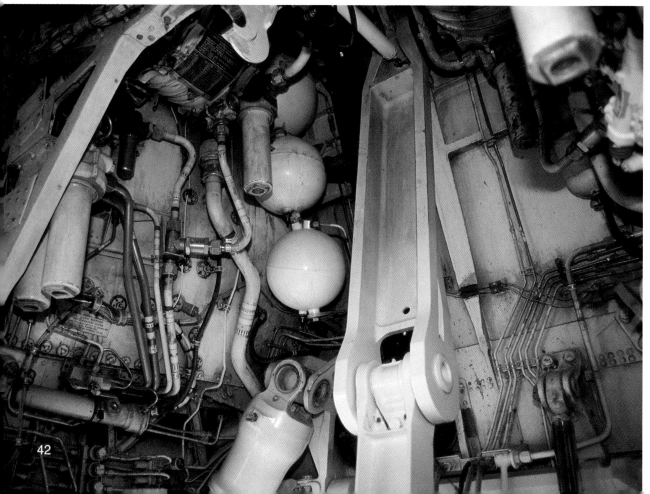

(Left top) The landing gear has an appearance of massively robust strength, which is entirely vindicated by its performance: the aircraft was originally intended to make carrier landings – just about the most abusive thing you can do to an aeroplane, short of flying it into a mountain.

(Left bottom) Inside the main gear wheel well: a maze of fluid lines, cable sheaves, bottles, trunions, braces and related components.

Despite the noise of the engines and the start cart, the cockpit crew and the ground crew can communicate right up until the time the aircraft leaves the parking spot thanks to the intercom system modelled here by a crew chief.

The Aardvark will haul all of these devices, but not all at once. This layout in front of an FB-111A of the 509th BW includes just about everything in the arsenal, including some 'nukes' – B28 free-fall bombs, and B43 tactical devices. *(Ken Hammond/USAF/Arms Communications)*

Mk 84 Mod O GP 2,000 lb bomb
clamped to the inboard pylon. The
F-111 can carry up to 33,000 lbs of
assorted 'pig iron', cluster bombs,
nukes, and precision munitions on
the wings and in the internal bomb
bay – unless the bomb bay is filled
with a Pave Tack pod, which the
Foxtrot models normally employ.

During actual combat operations
success can depend on the ability of
the ground crews to rapidly refuel
and rearm aircraft returned from a
strike so that they can be launched
again with minimum delay. One of the
essential skills for the ground teams
is the 'integrated combat turn', a
carefully choreographed routine that
gets bombs and missiles loaded
aboard a jet with maximum speed
and efficiency. Here a crewman
hustles to complete the bomb loading
sequence for a Mk 84.

A full rack of Mk 82 GP 500 lb bombs, the blue paint identifying these as inert training rounds.

Pave Tack is a system fitted to the F model; this expands the ability of the Aardvark to hit the target night or day, fair weather or foul, with laser, television, or IR-guided precision munitions, along with the regular 'pig iron' and the area weapons. This ability to unleash the GBU-15 and its ilk is the reason that the F model was the main version to participate in the Gulf War – where it was a star performer, and suffered zero losses – although the E model did see action from the base at Incirlik, Turkey. The pod rotates for take-off and landing, keeping the vulnerable bits safe inside until well away from the abrasive qualities of the runway.

EF-111A Raven

Sharing the same basic airframe as the fighter/bomber version of the Aardvark, the EF-111A Raven is altogether a different beast. The Raven is an electronic countermeasures aircraft – a jammer – and while the exterior shows a strong family resemblance to the Aardvark the inside is radically different.

Ravens are conversions of old A models. A long canoe-shaped radome was added on the belly, accommodating the Raven's weapons: emitters for powerful communications jamming transmitters. A large housing was also added to the vertical stabilizer, and this is likewise stuffed with electronic

Forty-two of these EF-111A tactical jamming system aircraft were converted by Grumman from original F-111 Alphas. Each carries 6,000 lbs of AN/ALQ-99A electronics, the same system as in the EA-6B Prowler. Even back in the mid-1970s when they were converted the Raven was expensive, 'retailing' at $42 million a copy. *(Photo, Randy Jolly/Arms Communications)*

countermeasure antennae. The right-seater is an electronic warfare officer ('EWO'), and his flight controls have been entirely deleted. To replace them he has the controls for an AN/ALQ-99E jamming system, including ten transmitters, five emitters, and a radio frequency calibrator. These systems provide the capability to automatically detect, identify, and counter many hostile radar systems.

The ECM mission doesn't get a lot of attention, but it is tremendously important in the plan of battle. When a CBU-87 detonates on a strategic or tactical target it is spectacularly obvious that the enemy has been – as the planners like to say – 'abraded'. But the ECM mission is far more subtle and difficult to measure; it involves things *not* happening. By jamming radars the ECM crews suppress enemy forces by making it difficult or impossible for them to react effectively, but there will never be any dramatic videotape replay of somebody's radar getting jammed.

Theoretically, you can jam a system from land-based stations far from the battlefield. But the problem for electronic countermeasures is that it takes buckets of power to suppress a target system, and the farther away the suppressing emitter is, the more juice is required.

So the Raven is designed to get in close and to focus its power narrowly on very specific frequencies.

To do this efficiently the Raven's AN/ALQ-99 stores up data 'pictures' of known enemy threat frequencies, which the EWO uses for reference during a mission. When a target emitter is detected the Raven's crew can use the ALQ-99 to jam the enemy radar automatically or manually.

There are several basic Raven missions. One is to have a singleton or a pair of EF-111s accompany a 'strike package' attacking a target, providing an 'electronic smoke screen' to protect the fighter/bomber component of the mission. Another is to stand off, outside enemy territory, and suppress radars from a safe (although less effective) distance. Yet another involves putting several Ravens into an airspace and onto a set of target frequencies; their massed power can provide an opaque curtain, masking the activities of large formations of friendly aircraft.

Despite – or maybe because of – the age of these systems, the old Aardvark has converted its sceptics to ardent fans. As Major Tom Yanni says:

'We do pretty much everything in the ground attack role: offensive counter-air – attacking enemy airfields,

suppression of enemy air defences – we can go a long way, at low altitude, hide from the enemy radars down low, at the beginning of a campaign. Then later, when we've got rid of all those SAMs, we can go higher to get above the small arms fire and triple-A. We do classic interdiction: go way back into the enemy area to destroy rail yards, chemical production facilities, factories – deny the enemy the ability to supply and equip his front lines.

'Then we do what we call BAI, or battlefield aerial interdiction: deny the enemy the ability to influence the battle by (for example) taking out a tank column that's getting ready to road march toward the front.

'It used to be, until recently, that airplanes had very distinct missions and roles, but those distinctions have changed. What does the '111 do? We can carry just about every bomb in the inventory: Mk 82s, 84s, cluster bombs, combined effects munitions, gator mines, all the dumb bombs – as well as all the precision munitions, the 500 and 2,000 lb laser-guided bombs. While any of the '111s can drop the laser-guided munitions, only the F has the laser suite to designate targets.

'It gives you a *lot* of capabilities, especially the F model with precision-guided munitions. They've got new terrain following radars, attack radars; they've got a lot of hours left on the airframes, and the avionics have been redone. The planners looked at newer engines and wings, and decided they weren't needed – the existing ones are fine. I think it will be around for a long time, because it is an extremely versatile, long range airplane. When you start talking about 'global reach/global power', range is a factor. We need an airplane in our ground attack mix that has the legs to carry a respectable weapons load a long way; and that's what you get with the F-111.

'The F-111 hit every class of target in the Gulf War – suppression of enemy air defences, interdiction, strategic interdiction, BAI, close air support – everything except air-to-air. They hit everything, and they did *great*. I think it is viable, it adds something to the force mix ratio; if you took the F-111 away you would lose something important. It took a while to get the bugs ironed out, but now it is a super-reliable system. You can beat it up – it's tough; you can lose half your hydraulics and still fly the airplane home; you can fly it around with total electrical failure – it makes it a tough airplane to kill.'

The EF-111A Raven shows the family resemblance, but has an entirely different character. It is an electronic countermeasures (ECM) system designed to turn enemy radar displays into useless nonsense. That's accomplished by radiating vast quantities of radio energy from antennae on the belly and tail. All the EF-111As in this sequence hail from the 390th Electronic Combat Squadron based at Mountain Home AFB, Idaho. *(Both photos, Randy Jolly/Arms Communications)*

With the wings fully aft (72 degrees) and up at altitude the Raven can achieve the same Mach 2.5+ speeds as the Aardvark. The sweep system is essentially a very simple screw drive mechanism connected to a sliding control above the pilot's throttle: slide the control aft, and the wings smoothly pivot back in unison. *(Photo, Randy Jolly/Arms Communications)*

3: How to Fly the F-111

The Aardvark is not particularly difficult to get airborne, and like most military aircraft the start sequence is very simple. The hard part – the part that requires years of training and experience – is using the aeroplane effectively and efficiently, executing missions and dealing with emergencies with good judgement. The routine things are simple.

Settle yourself down in the left seat and strap in; put on your helmet, connect the oxygen mask and the plugs for the headset and mike. Routine engine starts are done with the aid of a 'start cart', supplying electrical power and enough hot air for a political convention. The normal routine fires Number Two (on the right) first. On the ground check panel in the centre console will be found the 'ground ignition' control; switch it to PNEUMATIC and the system will be configured to spin the engine with air from the start cart. The flight control computers are also energized. Signal the ground crew to start their engine by bringing your right fist against your left palm. Now, lift

the Number Two throttle handle and hold it extended; although the throttle is fully aft in the STOP position, this permits the air from the cart to start spinning the compressor section. When the RPM indicates 19 per cent, turbine inlet temperature is below 100, and the oil pressure indicator comes off the stop, the hydraulic pressure warning on the master caution panel goes out – then push the throttle forward over the detent to IDLE. Without any more input from you the engine should light off, and you'll know when that happens because the RPM gauge will start to unwind, TIT will start to climb toward the green range, and you can feel and hear it through the spine of the airframe.

Signal the ground crew to pull the electrical and pneumatic power and the nose wheel pins, and to make the routine checks to ensure everything's healthy. Disengage the pneumatic switch on the ground start console, and repeat the process for the left 'powerboat'.

With both engines alive and kicking, the right-seater will work through his checklist, the most crucial and time-consuming part of which is initializing the inertial navigation system (INS). This can take up to 25 minutes, but since it provides the foundation for extremely accurate navigation the delay is worth while. Finally, with checklist completed, you're ready to taxi.

Listen to the prerecorded ATIS broadcast with its current information about winds, visibilities, and active runways; then call ground: 'Cannon Ground, BULLY ONE, taxi, one hound, with information OSCAR.' 'BULLY ONE, taxi to Runway Two Two' comes the reply in the headset, and you're free to release brakes and trundle down to the arming area just short of the runway. Here a team of specialists swarm around the

Captain Alex Pruitt serves with the 524th TFTS and the Standards and Evaluation group at Cannon, and makes frequent check rides to evaluate the proficiency of crew members. Here he plays his role in planning a four-ship mission. Mission planning and preparation take more time on the ground than most missions spend in the air – which is just as well, because when things go wrong they do so in a hurry, with nasty consequences for mistakes. Flight planning includes anticipating what to do if any of a hundred things happen. On this particular flight one of the aircraft suffered a bird-strike, a potentially disastrous problem that this time resulted in only slight damage to the F-111.

jet, pulling the pins that keep the bombs from falling off the racks or the missiles from sizzling through the parking area by accident. When they finally pronounce you fit to fly, call the tower: 'Cannon tower, BULLY ONE, number one for Runway Two Two.'

You get cleared to the active, and roll out and into position; for normal four-ship formation departures the lead will roll down to the first 1,000 ft marker. He'll advance his throttles to the 'MIL' power setting, and by doing so causes the ground spoilers on the wings to retract – the usual signal for the others in the flight to run up and check their engines.

The throttles are now advanced to 'burner for a quick check, then retarded to MIL power again. If nobody in the flight complains, lead will go into 'burner again, and start his take-off roll. Getting the '111 airborne from this point is entirely straightforward: throttles full forward, release the toe brakes, and you start rolling. Track the centreline with the rudder pedals (which are linked to the nose wheel at low speeds, the rudder at higher); stay off the grass, and watch the airspeed indicator unwind. At 142 knots move the stick aft until the nose lifts to an indicated ten degrees, and keep it there. The aircraft will normally come right up into the air with a nice rate of climb – but if it doesn't get off by 157 knots, abort the take-off, because something's wrong. Assuming a positive rate of climb, retract the gear and flaps, lower the nose a little to build the airspeed, and you have successfully 'slipped the surly bonds of earth'.

'Eject, Eject!'

Despite the best efforts of designers, builders, maintenance crews, and pilots themselves, aeroplanes inevitably fail their crews from time to time. When that happens there are really only two choices: ride it down, or abandon it in the air.

Over the years a small number of Aardvarks have been abandoned aloft due to engine failures, bird-strikes, or controls that cease to function. When a catastrophe strikes the crew have to make crucial decisions – quickly. At low level attack airspeeds the jet will be moving about 1,000 ft each second; if it is moving vertically toward the ground, each second's hesitation brings the crew 1,000 ft closer to death.

It isn't difficult to punch out (unless the aircraft is in a high-G spin): all you do is grasp one of the yellow handles on the centre console, squeeze the grip firmly, and pull. After a delay of .2 seconds your harness will pull you back hard against the seat, and you will hear a roar so loud you think your eardrums have burst – and they may have. A cord of explosive will detonate, cutting the cockpit capsule away from the fuselage. Then a rocket motor will fire, lifting the capsule up and away from the remainder of the carcass; small sections of the wing remain attached in order to stabilize the capsule. A drogue 'chute deploys, slowing the flight of the aluminium box. Depending on the altitude of the ejection, the 'chute canopy will deploy fully when the

automatic sensors determine it is safe (although the pilots have the ability to do it manually, too). Sometimes, as was recently the case with a crew from Cannon, you may be treated to the sight of your aircraft impacting the ground and forming a lovely fireball while you are still seated in the separated cockpit.

Although the ejection system works reliably, and is obviously preferable to the experience of impacting terra firma, ejecting is not exactly a fun experience. It is very noisy; you get loaded with 14 Gs; and when the capsule finally returns to earth, the impact (despite the canopy above and the air bag below) is enough to crack and compress vertebrae – one of life's more memorable experiences. The really hard part, however, is explaining to the investigators exactly why you felt compelled to waste millions of dollars of taxpayers' money.

Landing the Aardvark

Getting yourself into the air is a relative piece of cake, but getting down again without bending the machine is a different matter. Start by finding the airfield and listening to the prerecorded ATIS information; then proceed by calling the tower to let them know you will be dropping by: 'Cannon tower, BULLY ONE with information WHISKEY for initial Runway Two-Two'. They will call back with your clearance.

There are several kinds of approaches, but the easiest is a simple straight-in landing. At ten miles you should have positioned yourself on the runway axis; power back and decelerate to about 250 knots, then lower the gear and flaps at about 220 knots. By then you will be about five or six miles out, descending at 200 knots. A power setting of about 85 to 90 per cent will sustain level flight. The final approach is done at a basic airspeed of 130 knots, plus one knot for each 1,000 lbs of stores (7,000 lbs of stores would add seven knots to the approach speed).

But airspeed is less important when landing a 'Ground Pig' than angle of attack, which should be ten units of 'alpha', as they call it. 'It's hard to describe, but after you've flown the Aardvark for a while you just know when you've got the right alpha', says Capt. Bill Leake, an instructor pilot with the 524th Tactical Fighter Training Squadron. 'It settles – it feels like the back end is falling out from underneath you . . . it settles into a kind of notch, and you're at the right attitude. As with any aircraft, you want to take your time setting it up; but when you find that notch, bump the power up a little to maintain that alpha, and ride it down.'

There are some aeroplanes that you can land in a crab, and many that need to be slid gently back on the concrete; but not the '111. You want to have it pointed straight down the centreline, and you want to thump it back down firmly. Don't try to flare it, and don't be gentle. Plant the wheels 500 ft down the strip, right at the numbers, hard enough to compress the struts. The landing gear looks like it was made of cast iron (wheels included), and was originally designed for carrier recoveries. 'A good landing looks rough on the outside but feels smooth in the cockpit,' Captain Leake advises.

* * *

So: it's a good, mature, capable combat aircraft with lots of virtues and a few vices. Its technologies are mostly not state-of-the-art, but the bugs have been worked out of them. The cockpit is a bit cluttered, but it works. The eletronics are sometimes more analogue than digital; but the bombs seem to land on the bunkers farther from the bases than other, more 'gee-whiz' aircraft can deliver them. It's a great aeroplane.

Paperwork. . . . You can't go play with the taxpayers' toys until you've done your homework, and signed your name about 20 times.

All aircrew have 'bowling bags', used for carrying helmets, oxygen masks and assorted flying kit. They also serve as a highly visible 'curriculum vitae', as jet jocks invariably plaster them with patches from their former units.

Although the crew chief will have thoroughly inspected and prepared the aircraft, nobody goes flying without a walkaround inspection, just to make sure. Normally it begins at the boarding ladder and continues in a clockwise direction all the way around the aircraft in a sequence detailed in the checklist. All pins pulled? Any loose fittings, panels, bombs? Any tools left in the engine? No matter who left them there, if the pilot launches with a defect he should have caught, it's his fault.

It may not be graceful, but this is the easy way to shuffle an aircraft around the ramp area. Aircraft are frequently moved from one facility to another – to the paint shop, to a hanger for a major inspection, to the engine facility. It's slow, but it saves on gas.

Bombs, in particular, are inspected carefully for security. As long as they are supposed to be attached to the airframe you want them attached firmly, with no slack and no loose bits; but when you want them to leave, they should be ready to leave forever, in a hurry. Even so, aircraft will sometimes have weapons hang up and refuse to drop – or, worse, have bombs drop unexpectedly. Both events can be the result of improper loading and an inadequate preflight.

Pulled over to the side of the taxiway with the hood up and the guys from the AAA (American Aardvark Association) trying to figure out why it won't go. The tech has a portable diagnostic unit plugged in.

A ground crew member stands by during the start sequence with Halon, just in case. 'Hot' starts do happen, although normally without disastrous consequences.

(Left) As the engines spin up and light off the crew chief takes a look to insure that nothing is rattling around in the intake, no blades are falling off, or puddles of fuel catching fire in inappropriate ways.

(Above & below) A 522nd TFS 'whizzo' works through his lengthy pre-taxi checks; his left-seater watches the clocks and listens in to ATIS for weather and runway status. The Aardvark's inertial navigation system (INS) takes up to 25 minutes to initialize.

Finally. . . all the aircraft are good to go, all the lights on the Master Caution panel go out, all the needles point to green arcs, the radios work, and nothing has fallen out of the tail pipe.

PLASTIC TRANSPARENCIES
INSTALLED CONSULT
T.O. IF-111A-2-2-1
FOR SPECIAL CARE

Ground crews complete routine maintenance on a D model of the 428th TFTS 'Buccaneers' after a training sortie.

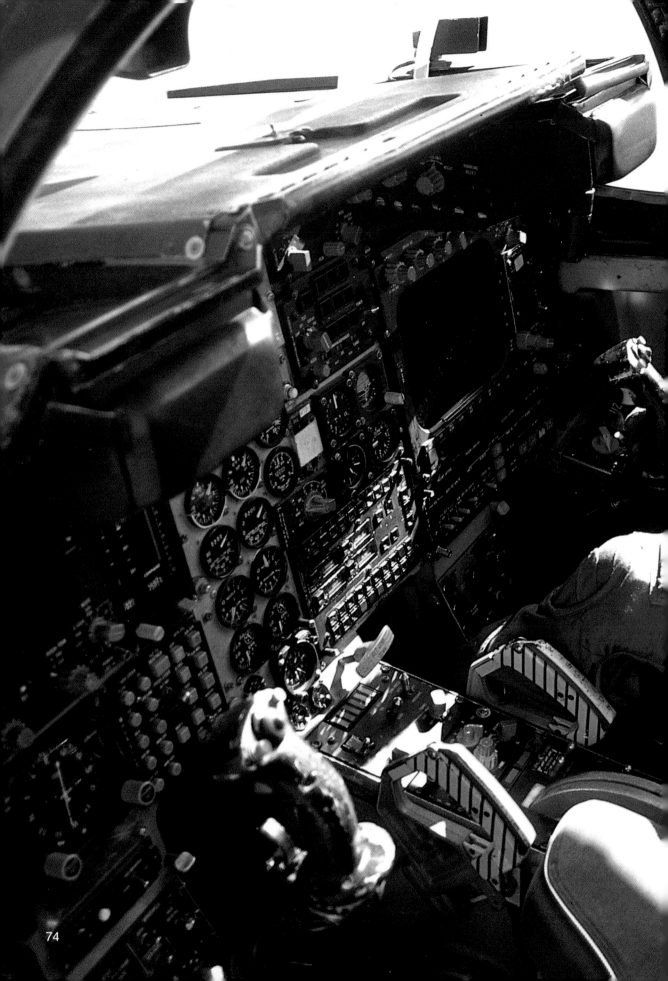

Major Tom Yanni, 524th Tactical Fighter Training Squadron 'whizzo extraordinaire', in his place of work.

The pilot's side has the usual stuff in the usual places, but with the addition of a wing sweep control above the throttles.

The radar altimeter, a particularly useful device in an aircraft that spends a lot of time less than 100 ft above the deck at 500+ knots.

Ribbon gauges above the Master Caution panel display angle of attack, Mach, and indicated air speed.

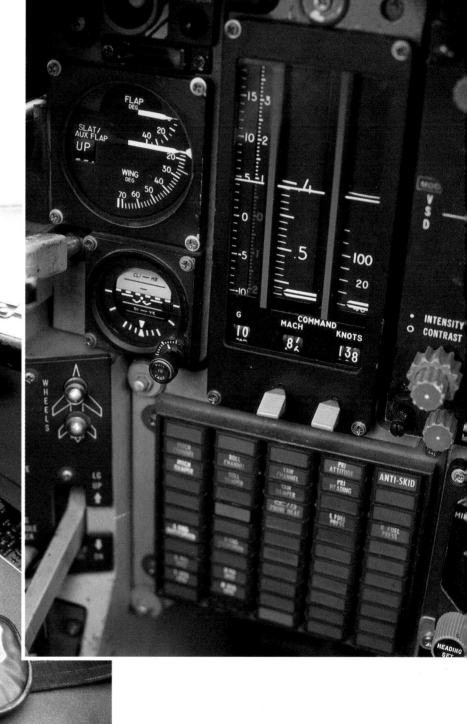

It's true what they say about the cockpit of the F-111: there is just about the same amount of room available as in a 1961 MG Midget (though with rather more instrumentation, and better rain-proofing).

There is little nose art on Aardvarks, but a select few are graced with decorations on the instrument panels, like the squadron commander's jet of the 522nd TFS. 'Miss Fireball Annie' is part of the squadron's legend and lore.
In addition to 'Annie' the squadron has other traditions as well: a red bowling ball, the official squadron 'fireball', is kept by one of the officers for at least five – but no more than 22 – days, after which he and several

The WSO's radar (with a test screen displayed here) is the heart of the D model's mission capability. The radar will provide enough information to identify and engage targets on the ground, in ghastly weather and on the darkest night. It enables the weapon systems officer to largely automate part of the final delivery sequence for weapons, offering enhanced precision. It is designed to aim 'dumb' bombs, however, not the precision weapons that use terminal guidance designation systems.

friends of his choosing execute a 'no-notice' transfer to some other officer in the unit. The receiving officer has no more than five minutes and 22 seconds to provide the guests with the drinks of their choice. Other squadrons maintain similar traditions, including one that carries around a big blue rock; and the 428th TFTS 'Buccaneers' have a pirate flag and a skull and crossbones – real ones.

Wing sweep indicator, angle of attack, Mach and indicated air speed, to the left of the pilot's multi-function display.

The WSO gets to drive occasionally, so he has a stick just like his partner on the left. The red button releases whatever weapon has been selected; the conical one in the middle is the trim button; the white one is for engaging the autopilot.

The Master Caution panel can tell the crew stories they need to know but would really rather not hear: about engine fires, system failures at inopportune moments, battle damage, and more. Anybody who gets a ride in the full-motion simulator will hear these stories all too often: it's one place where the training staff can guarantee that anything that can go wrong, will.

Round glass analogue instruments like these are now considered out of date; the latest trend is the so-called 'glass cockpit', with a handful of large, multi-function displays, as in the F-15E Strike Eagle – a newer and somewhat competitive aircraft for the deep interdiction mission.

The harness system is different from other combat aircraft with ejection seats. The crews strap themselves firmly to the seats, rather than to a harness system that is a component of a parachute. Behind the headrest is a container for survival equipment and supplies.

(Below) The pin is still attached, so the capsule ejection system is safe. Having the handles here, rather than overhead or between the knees as in other systems, has advantages in a spin (and Aardvarks will spin): in either a left or a right spin, somebody's going to be able to get a hand on one of them and squeeze.

A/C 122
NOTE:
THIS KIT CONTAINS VITAL LIFE
SAVING DEVICES FOR AIRCREW
SURVIVAL. IT DOES NOT CONTAIN
FIREARMS OR NARCOTICS.

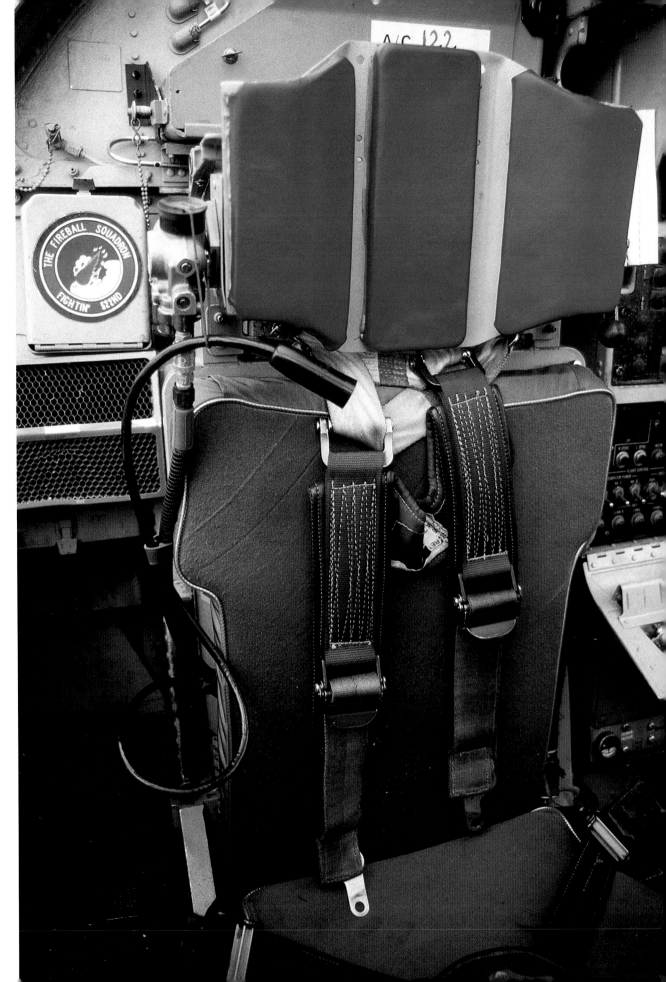

The splotchy camouflage is gradually being replaced by the all-grey scheme. For some reason paint schemes on military aircraft go through cycles of popularity: solids will be in for a while, then dark camouflage, then light, then solids again. After each change somebody declares that the new treatment is superior to the old.

The head up display (HUD) provides essential information to the pilot during situations (like low level penetration missions) when he needs a constant flow of information without taking his eyes off the road.

In late afternoon the ramp starts to fill up as all the flights of two and four return from a few hours of sightseeing around the south-western United States, and perhaps of dropping bombs on selected parts of it.

The F-111 is really a handsome design that has overcome its early problems to become a star performer in the force mix of the United States Air Force: fast, reliable, long-legged, versatile, stealthy, and strong, it has turned out to be an excellent investment for the long haul.

The full-colour Wing patch displayed under the cockpit of an Aardvark of the 'Fireballs'.

PLASTIC TRANSPAREN
INSTALLED CONSU
T.O. 1F-111A-2-2-
SPECIAL CARE

ARMAMENT

93

The Fighter Weapons School is based at Nellis Air Force Base near Las Vegas, Nevada, but sends people and aircraft all over. This emblem is displayed on a visiting F model that dropped in to Cannon for a short visit.

The emblem of the 27th Fighter Wing adorns the jet of its commander, Col. Alfred Franklin.

The emblem of the 522nd TFS.

This patch is worn by Captain 'Buffalo Bill' Leake, one of the 524th TFTS instructor pilots.

The 428th TFTS have gotten into the pirate business in a serious way; they fly the 'Jolly Roger', maintain a real skull in a pirate hat as a mascot, and wear this elaborate patch on their flight suits.